THE KREGEL PICTORIAL GUIDE TO THE OLD TESTAMENT

MICHAEL A. GRISANTI

CONTENTS

What Is the Old Testament?	3
A Chosen People	4
From a People to a Nation	6
Mediatorial Rulers: Judges and Kings	8
Divided Monarchy, Exile, and Return	10
Israel and the Mosaic Law	12
The Role and Impact of the Prophets	14
The Message of the Prophets	16
Poetry and Wisdom Literature	18
Religious Life	20
Religious Buildings	22
Religious Activity	24
Old Testament Covenants	26
The God of the Old Testament: Who Was He?	27
The God of the Old Testament: What Did He Do and What Did He Demand?	30
Further Reading	32
Index	32

Kregel Publications

Design copyright © 2001 Angus Hudson Ltd/Tim Dowley & Peter Wyart trading as Three's Company

Text copyright © 2009 Kregel Publications

Published in the United States in 2009 by Kregel Publications, a division of Kregel, Inc., P.O. Box 2607, Grand Rapids, Michigan, 49501.

ISBN 978-0-8254-2690-2

All rights reserved. No part of this publication may be reproduced, stored in a retrieval system, or transmitted in any form or by any means – for example, electronic, photocopy, recording – without the prior written permission of the publisher. The only exceptions are brief quotations in printed reviews.

Except for the verses quoted on pp. 19 & 28 (NRSV), all Scripture taken from the HOLY BIBLE, NEW INTERNATIONAL VERSION®, NIV®. Copyright © 1973, 1978, 1984 by International Bible Society. Used by permission of Zondervan Publishing House. All rights reserved.

Designed by Peter Wyart, Three's Company

Worldwide co-edition organized and produced by
Angus Hudson Ltd,
Concorde House,
Grenville Place, Mill Hill,
London NW7 3SA, England
Tel: +44 20 8959 3668
Fax: +44 20 8959 3678
e-mail: coed@angushudson.com

Printed in China

What is the Old Testament?

Here are four important issues:

1. Literary Focus
At the outset, the Old Testament involves thirty-nine books written by different authors and editors, some named but many unnamed. We regard all these books as given by God and authoritative. The Holy Spirit's ministry of "inspiration" (2 Tim. 3:16; 2 Peter 1:20–21) guarantees the accuracy and reliability of the contents of those Old Testament books.

2. Theocentric Focus
Most importantly, the Old Testament provides the reader of the Bible a very clear and vivid presentation of the character and activity of God. The Old Testament begins and ends with a focus on God as the orchestrator of far-reaching events. Although the Old Testament gives much attention to the nation of Israel and some attention to other parts of God's creation, God himself serves as the fount, sovereign, and goal of the Old Testament.

3. Theological Focus
When God created the universe he affirmed the divine intent to make man according to his image and to function as his image-bearer (Gen. 1:26–27). He designed mankind to bring the universe under subjection to his perfect rule. Although Adam and Eve's fall into sin marred that image, the rest of the Old Testament demonstrates how God will bring his plan to pass. His choice of Abraham to father a people is a fundamental step in executing that plan. The rest of the Old Testament develops God's use of Israel, both then and for the future, as a key part of his plan for the entire world.

4. Applicational Focus
Although many view the Old Testament as a "dark" section of

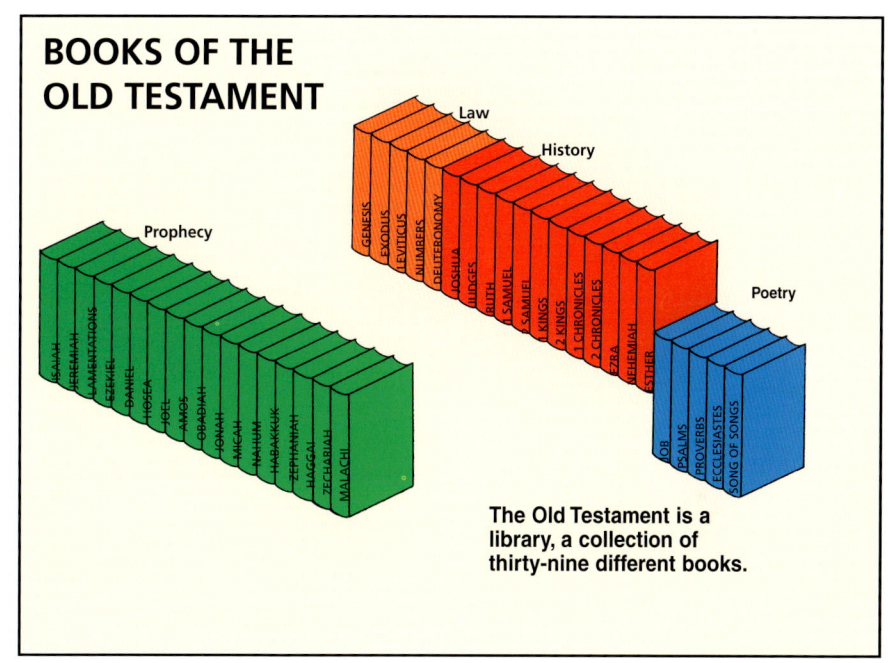

BOOKS OF THE OLD TESTAMENT

The Old Testament is a library, a collection of thirty-nine different books.

the Bible that is difficult to understand, it has continuing relevance for contemporary readers. Many New Testament images and concepts are predicated on Old Testament realities. The Old Testament also contains graphic narratives about God's dealings with Israel and the nations that are essential to a person's proper apprehension of God and his intentions for the world.

A Chosen People

The biblical events found in Genesis can be categorized as primeval (first) events (Gen. 1–11) and patriarchal history (Gen. 12–50—Abraham, Isaac, Jacob, and Joseph).

Primeval Events

The culmination of God's creation of the universe entailed his creation of Adam and Eve (Gen. 1–2). After some time, Adam and Eve chose to sin against God and were cast out of the Garden of Eden (Gen. 3). Their sin (Fall) marred the image of God in them and necessitated divine intervention in order for God's plan for the universe to find fulfillment. The deterioration of humanity into deep sin occasioned the need for the Flood, which left only eight humans as survivors, Noah, his three sons, and their wives. A number of centuries later, another rebellion at Babel caused God to confuse the languages and force the people to spread out into the world around Babel. In the wake of that rebellion and chaos, God raised up Abraham to begin his plan of extending his dominion over the world.

Abraham, the Father of a People

God called Abraham and his wife to leave their home in Ur to travel to Canaan and establish a new life there (Gen. 12:1). They obeyed God and headed west, without knowing their exact destination (Heb. 11:8). God promised that Abraham and his descendants would become a great nation/people, have a land, and be a blessing (Gen 12:2–3). This required that Abraham and Sarah have a son, something that did not happen for 25 years. After it was obvious to all that only God could do it, the Lord gave them a son—Isaac, a son of promise who would carry on the plan of God for the world.

Isaac, His Father's Son

Isaac's unique birth (after his mother was too old to bear children) is a testament to God's commitment to his promises. Isaac and Rebekah had twin sons after many years of barrenness (again demonstrating God's role in keeping covenant). In accordance with God's will, Jacob (rather than Esau) carried on God's covenant plan.

Jacob, the Deceiver

Jacob's name, as well as his conduct for the first decades of his life, matched the meaning of his name: "usurper" or "deceiver." After marrying Rachel and Leah and spending over 14 years away from Canaan, Jacob and his entourage returned home. There he reared his twelve sons and daughter. His two sons by Rachel, Joseph and Benjamin, were his favorites.

Joseph, the Advance Scout

As one of his father's favorite son's, Joseph experienced strained relationships with his brothers. Eventually, Joseph's brothers sold him as a slave to a caravan of traders heading for Egypt, where he was sold to an Egyptian officer named Potiphar. Later, he was unjustly sent to prison. Because he had correctly interpreted dreams of some fellow-prisoners, the Pharaoh asked Joseph to interpret a dream that had eluded all the royal officials. Joseph's correct interpretation not only helped Egypt survive the upcoming lengthy famine, but also prepared the way for the preservation of Joseph's family from the same famine as well as corruption by the Canaanites. All of Joseph's experiences from the time he was sold as a slave until he was exalted to a ranking ruler over Egypt surely seemed inequitable at the time he experienced. However, God orchestrated these events so Joseph could be an "advance scout" to prepare the way for his chosen people's tenure in the land of Egypt.

The family of Abraham

- **ABRAHAM** (Abram)
- **SARAH** (Sarai)
- **NAHOR** (Abraham's brother)
- **NAHOR** (Abraham's niece and sister-in-law)
- **BETHUEL** (Abraham's nephew)
- **ISAAC** (Abraham's son)
- **REBEKAH** (Abraham's grand-niece through Nahor Daughter-in-law through Isaac)
- **LABAN** (Abraham's grand-nephew Jacob's uncle and father-in-law through Rebekah)
- **ESAU** (Abraham's grandson)
- **JACOB** (Abraham's grandson)
- **LEAH** (Jacob's cousin and wife)
- **RACHEL** (Jacob's cousin and wife)

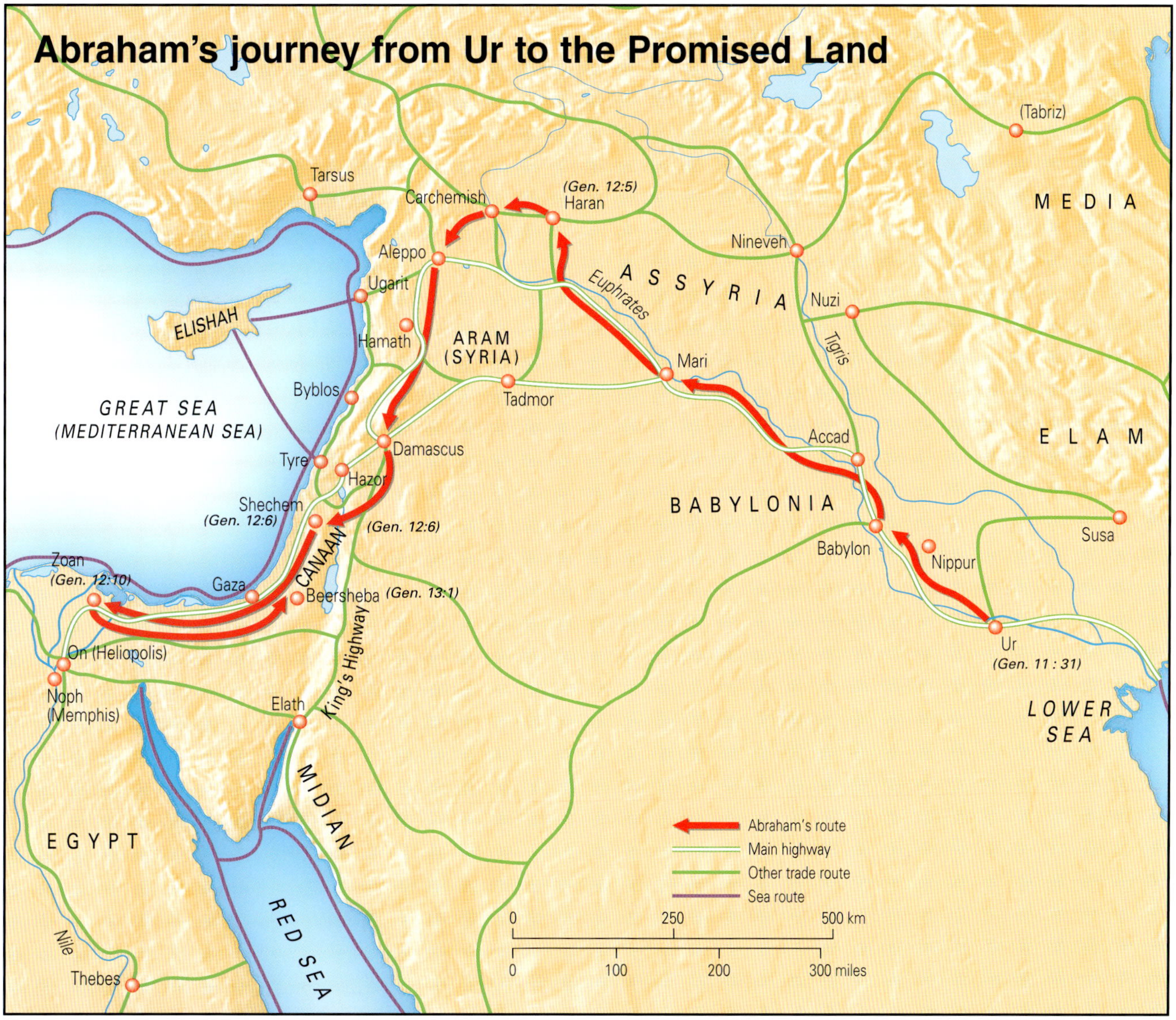

Abraham's journey from Ur to the Promised Land

The Cave of Machpelah, Hebron, burial place of Abraham's family.

Why did God choose the land of Canaan for the location of the Promised Land?

1. The land of Canaan was situated at an international crossroads. Geographically, the fact that this land was bounded by the Mediterranean Sea on the west and the Arabian Desert on the east created a "funnel" effect for all those traveling through this region. The distance between these two boundaries was rarely more than 100 miles.

2. As an international crossroads, major trade routes passed through this region, connecting the continents of Africa, Asia, and Europe. This would have brought the Israelites into contact with people from many other lands.

3. As a location for coveted trade routes, the land of Canaan would have been important for any regional power to control.

4. Since God commissioned the Israelites to make prominent his character to the surrounding nations (Exod. 19:4–6), he placed them in a place of great international significance. The land of Canaan was to function as a platform on which God's people could live out God's character before the numerous people with whom they would come into contact.

5. The land of Canaan was not a naturally productive area in general. Living in this region would never be easy. Consequently, what better place to put his chosen people than in a land where his people would be compelled to trust in the one and only true God of the universe as the only way for them to enjoy long tenure in that land.

From a People to a Nation

Israel's Sojourn in Egypt

For many years, Jacob and his descendants lived in the region of Goshen. However, a new king came to power in Egypt who had no connection to Joseph. He regarded the growing population of the Israelites as a growing threat, so he made them serve as Egyptian slaves. Later pharaohs passed decrees that required the execution of male babies to prevent the continued growth of these Hebrew. When Moses was born, all male babies were to be drowned in the Nile River. Moses' mother placed him in a woven basket in the Nile River, where an Egyptian princess found him. This princess raised Moses in the Egyptian palace, providing him all the training such a position could offer him. Eventually, Moses decided to identify with his fellow Hebrews. Once, when he intervened in a struggle between an Egyptian and a Hebrew, Moses accidentally killed the Egyptian. The pharaoh of that time (perhaps Thutmose III) pronounced the death penalty for Moses. Consequently, Moses fled into the wilderness region to the east of Egypt, where he would spend the next 40 years.

Israel's Exodus from Egypt

While in the wilderness, God commissioned Moses to lead his chosen people out of Egypt and to the land of promise (Exod. 3:1–12). Upon returning to Egypt, Moses exhorted the Pharaoh to allow the Hebrews to leave

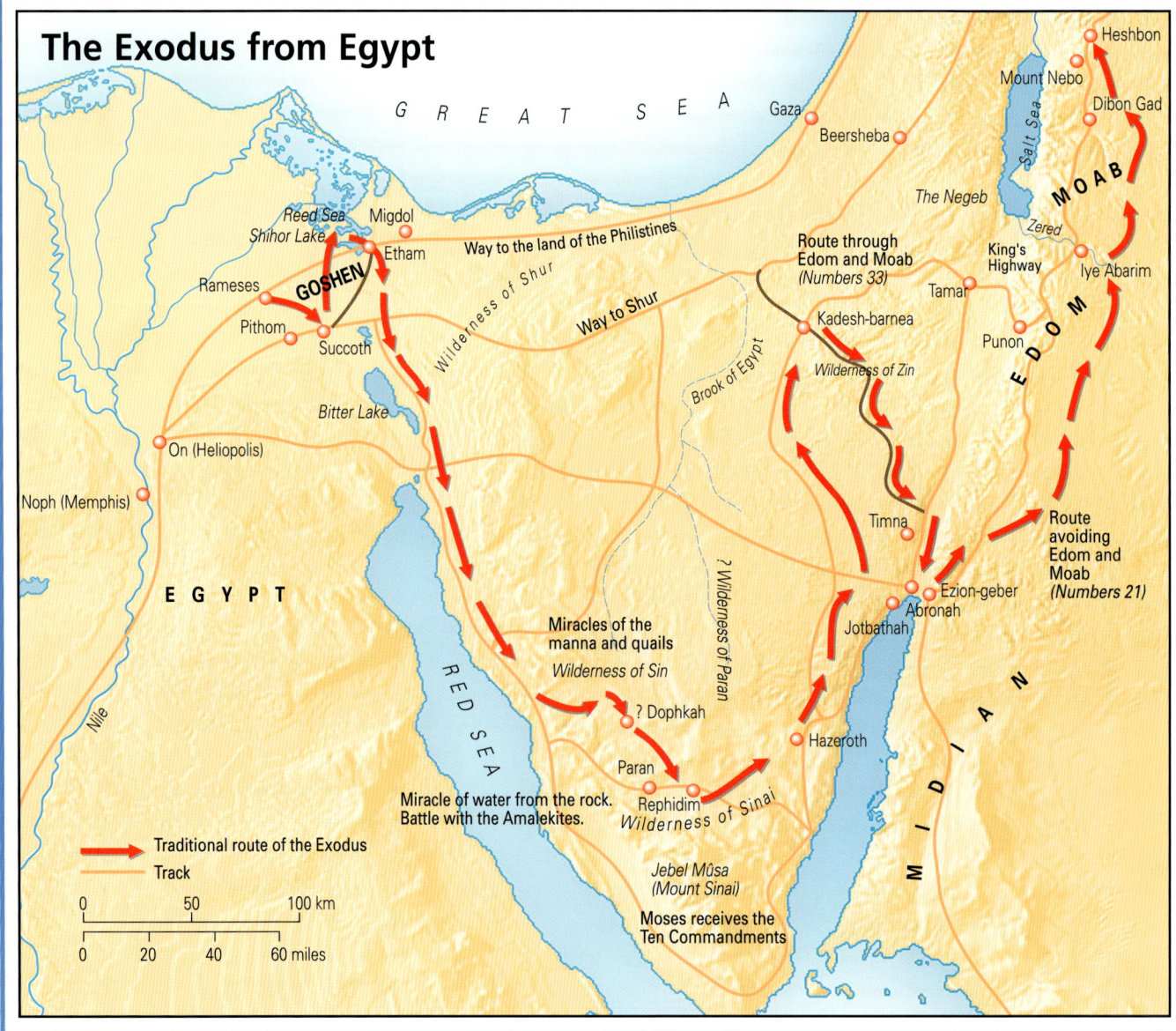

Basic Chronology of Sojourn in Wilderness

1/1/14	Arrival at the Wilderness of Sinai (Exod. 19:1)	
1/3/14	First Passover (Exod. 12:1–6)	2 mo.
2/2/20	Departure from Wilderness of Sinai (Num. 10:11–12)	11 mo., 6 days
40/11/1	Moses' Last Words (Deut. 1:3)	38 yrs., 8 mo., 11 days
41/1/10	Crossing of the Jordan (Josh. 4:19) **39 yrs. 11 mo. 26 days after the Passover	1 mo., 9 days
41/1/14	Celebration of the Passover (Josh. 5:10) **Exactly 40 years since the first Passover	4 days

Moses and his brother Aaron tell Pharaoh to release the Israelites from Egypt.

Egypt. The Pharaoh refused until twelve powerful plagues devastated many aspects of Egyptian life. A massive group of Israelites departed from Egypt, crossed the "Red Sea" through a stupendous miracle, and marched down the Sinai peninsula until they reached Mt. Sinai, where God gave his expectations (laws) to Israel through Moses (see below section for further explanation of Mosaic Law). After spending about eleven months camped at Sinai, the Israelites broke camp and traveled to Kadesh Barnea, a place from which they would enter the land of promise.

Wilderness Wandering

After refusing to enter the land of Canaan because of the reports of the might of the inhabitants, God punished Israel by requiring that the nation wander in the wilderness for almost forty years, until all the adults who had been alive at Kadesh Barnea perished. When that occurred, God directed the Israelites to begin their approach to the Promised Land, this time from the east side of the Jordan River. Just before they entered the land of Canaan, Moses died and Joshua replaced him as the leader of the nation of Israel.

Conquest of Canaan

Israel's crossing into the land of Canaan (through their miraculous crossing of the Jordan River at flood stage) represented a declaration of war against the city-states of Canaan. For the next seven years or so, the nation of Israel conquered the land of Canaan in three thrusts. By defeating Jericho they gained a foothold in the central region. Their defense of the Gibeonites and the ensuing victory gave them the upper hand in the southern region. Finally, their defeat of the northern alliance gave them control of the northern section as well. By the end of the Conquest proper, the nation of Israel was in control of the region generally, but had not rooted all the pockets of resistance (some sizable). That was the task of each tribe, with God's assistance. Joshua allotted the land of Canaan to the twelve tribes, in accordance with their population and God's direction. Unfortunately, even though God had demonstrated his love for the nation and had intervened on their behalf so many times, the nations was still characterized by unbelief (Josh. 24:14–28). Because of their refusal to completely trust in God, the Israelite tribes failed to evict the Canaanites that remained in their land allotments. That refusal led to the chaos that characterized the period of the Judges.

Key Practical Observations

1. God does exactly what he promises to do—God's promise to Abraham serves as the theological rationale for his facilitating Israel's Exodus from Egypt (Deut. 4:31). His servants can totally rely on him to keep his promises.

2. God is all-powerful—God intervenes in human history in incontestable ways, dividing the waters of the Red Sea and the flood waters of the Jordan River, to enable his chosen nation to carry out his plans for them. Through the ten plagues, he demonstrated his absolute supremacy over Egypt as well as the alleged gods of Egypt.

3. God is not to be trifled with—Rebellion against the covenant lord would occasion painful consequences. Disobedience of God's requirements represented much more than breaking a rule, but involved violating a dedicated relationship.

Mediatorial Rulers
Judges and Kings

Because of the failure of each Israelite tribe to evict the Canaanites from their tribal allotments, the nation of Israel experienced great moral chaos in the years after Joshua died. No national leader filled the void and the elders of the nation disappeared from the scene. Because of this absence of leadership and the penchant of the Israelites for rebellion, many Israelites married Canaanites and then began to practice their idolatry. This period of moral chaos would clearly demonstrate the need for God-appointed rulers who could lead the people as God demanded, i.e., kings. Even that venture, flawed by sin, did not measure up to God's expectations.

Judges
The judges of Israel (13 of them) were regional leaders (rather than national rulers) and had no dynastic rights (their sons did not automatically rule after they died). Sometimes, more than one judge ruled simultaneously over different areas. Each of the judges was somehow involved in leading Israel in throwing off the yoke of oppression of some foreign power. After they liberated the land of Israel, the judge would handle basic ruling functions for that region. They were enabled by God's spirit for this leadership role (theocratic anointing—Judg. 3:10; 6:34; 11:29; 14:6; 15:14). Throughout the book of Judges there is a pattern of sin, God sending judgment by means of a foreign oppressor, the nation crying out for deliverance, and God sending a judge/deliverer, and then after a period of peace, a return to rebellion.

Samuel: Transition from Judge to King
Although Samuel is called a judge (1 Sam. 7:15–17), he was more than a judge. He was primarily a prophet, so recognized from Dan to Beersheba (1 Sam. 3:20). In addition to this, he even acted as a priest (1 Sam. 9:12–13; 13:8–13). Samuel was also called to be a prophet and thus brought new revelatory activity (3:1–21; Acts 3:24). Toward the end of his life, the nation asked Samuel to anoint a king who could rule over them. They wanted a king like other nations had and wanted someone to lead them against a pressing enemy.

Saul
Although Saul was endorsed as God's choice for Israel's first king, Saul did not carry out his role in total obedience to God. Consequently, God affirmed that none of his sons would rule after him and then brought a premature end to his reign. In the midst of Saul's reign, God rejected Saul from the role of king and chose David, whom Samuel anointed, for that role. In the years that passed between that transition and Saul's actual death, David treated Saul with great respect.

David
David, called "a man after his own heart" (referring to Yahweh—1 Sam. 13:14) was born in Bethlehem and was the descendant of Boaz and Ruth (Ruth 4:17–22; Matt. 1:5). After Saul's death in battle, David became king and ruled over the tribe of Judah from Hebron (where he ruled for 72 years). The Philistines controlled Israelite land between those tribes and the tribes north and east of the hill country of Samaria and the Jezreel Valley. Ish-bosheth, a son of Saul, eventually ruled the rest of the tribes from Mahanaim in the Transjordan (after a period of chaos). After his assassination, the other Israelite tribes asked David to rule over all Israel. He chose Jerusalem as his capital, conquered the Jebusites who lived there, as well as the Philistines who rightly regarded him as a threat to their regional power. David was an impressive soldier and military leader, an effective king and diplomat, and a powerful poet (writing many psalms). Under his reign, the nation of Israel became a significant regional power. He led his army in conquering his

David defeated the Jebusite inhabitants and made Jerusalem his capital city.

But now your kingdom will not endure; the LORD has sought out a man after his own heart and appointed him leader of his people, because you have not kept the LORD's command.
1 Samuel 13:14

covenanted to have a Davidic descendant rule over Israel "forever" (2 Sam. 7:12–13), a promise that would culminate in the coming of Christ, "the son of David." At the end of his forty year reign, he delivered a stable kingdom over to his son, Solomon.

Solomon

After David's death, Solomon began his reign over Israel, drawing on the Lord's provision of wisdom (1 Kings 3:3–28). He was involved in various writing endeavors including psalms, proverbs, and perhaps Ecclesiastes and Song of Solomon. He conducted several significant building projects including building his palace as well as fortifying certain key Israelite cities, but most importantly, the Temple. As part

surrounding enemies or established treaties with them. His reign was not, however, without problems. He committed adultery with Bathsheba, arranged for the death of Bathsheba's husband (Uriah), and faced chaos within his own family. During his reign the Lord

Reading between the lines

One of the Holy Spirit's Old Testament ministries was *Theocratic Anointing*, which seems to have primarily involved administrative enablement (not an indication of the recipient's spiritual condition). After it was given to Moses, the elders, and Joshua (Num. 11:17–25; Deut 34:9), it was also given to the judges (four of whom are named: Othniel, Gideon, Jephthah, and Samson). It also came on Saul and David (1 Sam. 10:10); 16:13–14) and Solomon (1 Kings 3:7–12). Jesus also received this endowment at his baptism (Matt. 3:16).

of the burgeoning bureaucracy, Solomon divided the nation into twelve districts (that did not match tribal boundaries) for the purpose of taxation and conscription. During his reign, the people of Israelites felt the weight of supporting a kingdom grow significantly. As part of the political stability of Israel at this time, Solomon established a number of treaties with other regional powers, sealing some of those alliances with marriages between himself and foreign princesses.

Not only did his numerous alliances represent a lack of reliance on Yahweh for protection, but it also led to idolatry. Solomon built pagan temples for various foreign wives, located on a hill not far from the Temple mount (eventually called the Hill of Offense). Solomon's sponsoring of idolatrous worship perpetuated and deepened Israel's struggle with worshipping Yahweh alone, something that would manifest itself for centuries to come. As with many kings that followed him, it can be said that Solomon began well but ended badly. By the time of his death, he had lost control of Edom and Syria and fell out of favor with Egypt.

The Kingdoms of Israel and Judah

Divided Monarchy, Exile, and Return

Divided Monarchy
After Solomon's death and his son's (Rehoboam) decision to increase taxation of Israelites, inter-tribal tensions exploded into civil war. The ten northern tribes rejected Rehoboam as their king and formed their own nation (called Israel or the northern kingdom) and installed Jeroboam I as their king. Rehoboam continued ruling over the southern two tribes (called Judah or the southern kingdom).

Northern Kingdom
The northern kingdom had nineteen kings, but none were Davidic descendants and all of them ruled without regard for Yahweh. The prophets Elijah, Elisha, Hosea, Amos, and Jonah preached to the inhabitants of this nation. Eventually, because of their vile sin against Yahweh (cf. 2 Kings 17), the Lord allowed the Assyrian empire to subjugate these tribes and scatter them throughout the Assyrian empire (722 B.C.).

Southern Kingdom
The southern kingdom involved twenty kings, eight of which were "righteous" (some begun well but ended badly) and twelve were wicked. The good kings were evaluated as doing what was "right in the eyes of the Lord" (1 Kings 5:5) or ruling like David had (1 Kings 15:11). Isaiah and Micah are two of the key prophets who called God's people to repent and renew their commitment to their covenant relationship with Yahweh. The southern kingdom also exhausted God's patience through their penchant for rebellion. Babylon had replaced Assyria as the major power of the Ancient Near East and subjugated Judah, along with other nations in that region. They eventually destroyed Jerusalem and took a large number of Israelites as captives to Babylon (586 B.C.). After this exile to Babylon, Israel (God's chosen nation) had no national presence in the land of promise.

Exile to Babylon
Judah's exile to Babylon took place in three phases. In 605 B.C. the Babylonians took Daniel and his friends captive (Dan. 1:1, 10). In 597 B.C. Jehoiachin, the queen mother, Ezekiel, and ten thousand others were also deported. The prophet Ezekiel conducted his ministry to his fellow exiles up until and after the fall of Jerusalem. The final deportation occurred after Jerusalem was captured and destroyed (586 B.C.; 2 Kings 25:1–21).

During exile in Babylon, many of the distinctively Jewish institutions were maintained—elders, prophets, priests, feast days, etc. The exiled Jews enjoyed freedom of movement. Many had their own homes (Ezek. 8) and were able to correspond with friends back in Judah (Jer. 29:1, 25). There were also many employment opportunities. Nebuchadnezzar intentionally took many craftsmen and artisans in his exile of the Jews (2 Kings 24:14–16). Several enjoyed prosperous positions in commerce and government (e.g. Esther, Nehemiah, Daniel, et al.). Since many of the Jews lived by the river Chebar (Ezek. 1:1, 3; 3:15, 23), farming was the trade of many. Still, the exile was a form of punishment. The Israelites were uprooted from all

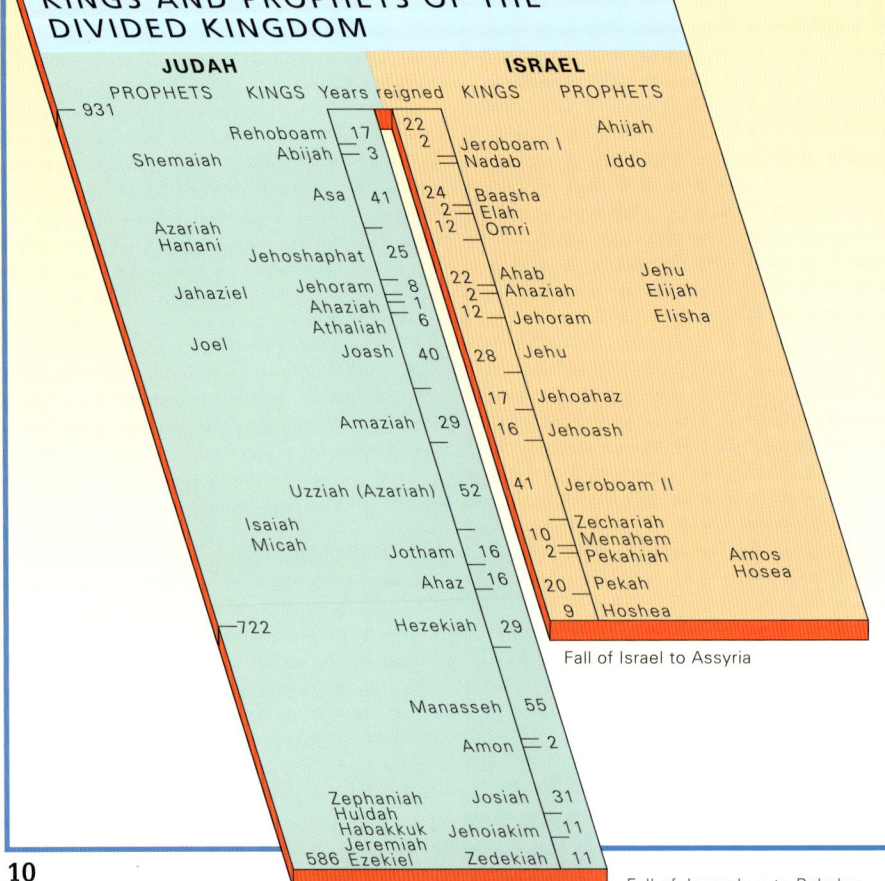

Fall of Israel to Assyria

Fall of Jerusalem to Babylon

The walls of Jerusalem were rebuilt under the leadership of Nehemiah.

Speak tenderly to Jerusalem, and proclaim to her that her hard service has been completed, that her sin has been paid for . . .
Isaiah 40:2

they knew and loved, were humiliated by being deported as captives, and lost all of their possessions.

Fall of Babylon to Medo-Persia

The Medes and Persians became one empire under the dominion of Cyrus the Great. Cyrus began his quest for regional domination by attacking and conquering areas that had been under Babylonian rule as well as some peoples outside of the Babylonian empire. Eventually he turned his attention to Babylon and was able to conquer the capital city with little loss of life. The Babylonian inhabitants, unhappy with their present rulers (Nabonidus and Belshazzar), welcomed Cyrus as they would a conqueror returning home.

The First Israelite Return

Soon after he conquered Babylon, Cyrus instituted a policy of encouraging exiled peoples to return to their homelands, allowing them to take their treasured religious vessels. Regardless, many Israelites chose to stay in Babylon. Zerubbabel and Joshua led about 50,000 Israelites on the first return to the land of promise (Ezra 1–6). They began rebuilding the Temple (536 B.C.) immediately. However, opposition

Babylonian infantryman.

by people who lived in that area ("Samaritans"—ethnic mixture of Israelites and non-Israelites) caused the Israelites to give up on building the Temple. After sixteen years of neglect, and in the wake of the prophetic exhortations of Haggai and Zechariah (520 B.C.), the Israelites returned to that important task and completed the Temple in 516 B.C.

Esther in Persia

Between the times of the first and second Israelite returns, Esther becomes the queen and plays a significant role in sparing her fellow Israelites from slaughter. The modern Feast of Purim celebrates that great deliverance.

The Second Israelite Return

Under Ezra's leadership (ca. 458 B.C.; Ezra 7–10), a couple of thousand more Jews made the pilgrimage from Babylon to Israel. After arriving in Jerusalem, Ezra sought to restore proper worship of Yahweh.

The Third Israelite Return

Nehemiah became burdened with the broken down condition of the walls of Jerusalem and returned to that beloved city to give direction to rebuilding those walls (ca. 444 B.C.; Neh. 1–13). After surveying the damage, the people were able finish the walls in a mere fifty-two days (Neh. 6:15).

Israel and the Mosaic Law

Historical Context

When Moses led the Israelites out of Egypt and the people began their journey toward the land of promise, they were a people without a clear identity and purpose. They left behind an Egyptian sojourn of 430 years. At the Red Sea, the Lord orchestrated one of the most stupendous miracles of the Old Testament. The Israelite crossing of this body of water on dry ground represented Yahweh's commitment to bring to pass what he had promised to his people and served as a paradigm for God's character and activity in the rest of the Old Testament. Once the people camped at the base of Mount Sinai, Yahweh led Israel to a greater depth in their relationship with him.

Ten Commandments: Core of the Law (Yahweh's Covenant Expectations)

Moses ascended Mount Sinai as Israel's representative to receive the Law from Yahweh. The Lord himself etched the words of the Ten Commandments on two stone tablets. These ten far-reaching divine requirements represented the heart of what Yahweh expected of his people. The first four commandments focus on an Israelite's relationship with God (vertical) while the other six commandments give attention to one's relationship with fellow Israelites (horizontal). It is important to notice that the Ten Commandments begin with a preface, something common in Ancient Near Eastern treaties. This preface or prologue generally provides the past dealings of the parties of the treaty. In this passage, the prologue demonstrates that God did not deliver his covenant demands to Israel in a vacuum, but in the context of an intimate relationship, clearly evidenced by his character and activity on Israel's behalf.

Detailed Legislation: Delineation of the Ten Commandments

The detailed rules and regulations that fill much of Exodus, Leviticus, and Deuteronomy are not a free-floating set of rules that have no connection with the Ten Commandments. Rather, they represent the detailed application of the character of God to every area of an Israelite's life. Furthermore, these regulations operate in two basic spheres: vertical and horizontal (cf. Christ's summary of the Mosaic Law into two spheres—Luke 10:25–28). Some laws, primarily those concerning the worship ritual and requirements that do not directly impact fellow Israelites (dietary regulations) focus on an Israelite's walk with God. They can be summed up as a call to live a life of total allegiance before Yahweh. Other laws concern the way an Israelite should treat their fellow citizens. In summary, God's chosen people are to treat each other with love, justice, and equity.

Rationale for the Law

What does it mean to be God's people? According to Exodus 19:4, Yahweh was solely responsible for delivering the Israelites from Egypt and bringing them to Mount Sinai. Concerning the covenant he is about to establish with them, he firmly connects their obedience with their ability to function as a witness nation before the world (Exod. 19:5–6). As a treasured possession, holy nation, and a kingdom of priests, they can represent God to the surrounding nations.

St Catherine's Monastery, near Mount Sinai, Egypt.

THE TEN COMMANDMENTS

And God spoke all these words: I am the LORD your God, who brought you out of Egypt, out of the land of slavery. You shall have no other gods before me. You shall not make for yourself an idol in the form of anything in heaven above or on the earth beneath or in the waters below.

You shall not bow down to them or worship them; for I, the LORD your God, am a jealous God, punishing the children for the sin of the fathers to the third and fourth generation of those who hate me, but showing love to a thousand [generations] of those who love me and keep my commandments. You shall not misuse the name of the LORD your God, for the LORD will not hold anyone guiltless who misuses his name. Remember the Sabbath day by keeping it holy. Six days you shall labour and do all your work, but the seventh day is a Sabbath to the LORD your God. On it you shall not do any work, neither you, nor your son or daughter, nor your manservant or maidservant, nor your animals, nor the alien within your gates. For in six days the LORD made the heavens and the earth, the sea, and all that is in them, but he rested on the seventh day. Therefore the LORD blessed the Sabbath day and made it holy. Honour your father and your mother, so that you may live long in the land the LORD your God is giving you. You shall not murder. You shall not commit adultery. You shall not steal. You shall not give false testimony against your neighbour. You shall not covet your neighbour's house. You shall not covet your neighbour's wife, or his manservant or maidservant, his ox or donkey, or anything that belongs to your neighbour.

Exodus 20:1–17

Now if you obey me fully and keep my covenant, then out of all nations you will be my treasured possession. Although the whole earth is mine, you will be for me a kingdom of priests and a holy nation.
Exod. 19:5–6a

The Role and Impact of the Prophets

What we call Old Testament prophecy is not identical with what the Jews regarded as prophecy. For them, the books of Joshua through 2 Kings were called "the Former Prophets" and Isaiah, Jeremiah, and Ezekiel were the latter prophets, along with "the Twelve" (the latter regarded as one book). The Jews also categorized the book of Daniel in the "Writings" (as opposed to the "Law" or the "Prophets"), possibly because he was a government official by vocation rather than a prophet.

Although the genre of prophetic literature has been found in other ANE bodies of literature, it is a category of literature with which we are not all that familiar. We have read and heard stories (narrative), sung songs (Psalms), and read letters (epistles), but we have not had a lot of exposure to prophetic writing outside the Bible. That "foreignness" of prophetic literature demands that we understand this kind of literature better.

The Prophetic Office
Although prophets did not play a significant role in Israel's history until the time of Samuel (who started the "band of prophets" 1 Sam. 10; 19), Moses provided the first extended discussion of a biblical prophet (Deut. 18:14–22), a passage that depicts as a prophetic paradigm. The institution of the prophetic office coincided with the establishment of Israel as Yahweh's covenant people at Sinai. Micaiah's words spoken to King Ahab, "As sure as the Lord lives, I can tell him only what the Lord tells me" (1 Kings 22:14; cf. 2 Chron. 18:13), provides a classic definition of a biblical prophet. Their message was not their own, but was based on the Mosaic Covenant and directed by God himself.

False Prophets
Unlike true prophets, false ones spoke a message that God did not endorse. The Israelites were to put to death any prophet who spoke presumptuously, as if God was speaking through them. The primary criterion for determining this was whether the prophetic statement came to pass (Deut. 18:21–22; cf. Jer. 28:15–17). If that was not possible, a prophet's pronouncement had to cohere with the message of the Torah (cf. Deut. 13:1–5; Isa. 8:19–20) and with the pronouncements of earlier prophets (Jer. 26:18–19; 28:8–9).

The Prophet's Use of Poetic and Figurative Language
The prophets use poetry for much of their message. In addition to parallelism, biblical poetry includes an extensive use of figures of speech and various kinds of graphic imagery. For example, rather than saying God is angry, they write "The lion has roared" (Amos 3:8). They graphically refer to Israel's rebellion by likening the nation's conduct to prostitution (Jer. 3:1c).

The Prophets and the Mosaic Covenant

- **They were messengers sent by God.** They were primarily preachers of God's message (Jer. 18:18; 27:18) and the conduits for divine revelation (Isa. 1:1; 2:1; Ezek. 7:26). The "word of the Lord" was something that "came" to them (Jer. 1:2, 4; 2:1), was within them (Hab. 2:1), and was spoken to them by Yahweh (Jer. 46:13). The Lord himself would bring to fulfillment what a prophet declared (Ezek 33:33; Dan 9:24). He gives careful attention to see that his words come true (Jer. 1:12) and that what he says will be done (Ezek. 12:25, 28).

- **They were sent to enforce Israel's allegiance to the covenant with Yahweh.** It is imperative to understand the biblical prophets against the backdrop of Israel's covenant relationship with Yahweh. Through the biblical prophets Yahweh reminds his chosen nation that he expects them to live in heartfelt conformity to the demands of this covenant demands.

Elijah struggles with the priests of Baal.

According to the prophets, Yahweh will abundantly bless their obedience and forcefully curse their disobedience (Lev. 26; Deut. 4; 28–32). The prophetic message draws heavily on the language of the Mosaic Covenant, esp. the wording found in the book of Deuteronomy. The prophets did not announce something new, but exhorting Israel to live in submission to the covenant to which they had given their allegiance (Exod. 19:7–8). In general, they served in *"covenant enforcement"* role or as *"prosecuting attorneys."* As God's chosen nation would turn away from him, forgetting this covenant commitment to which they had solemnly agreed, the prophets emerged as God's spokesmen to call the people back to covenant obedience.

Elijah's successor as prophet of Israel, Elisha was renowned for his miracle-working ministry.

This combination of poetry and figurative language uniquely impacts the emotions of the reader or listener.

Prophetic Books as Anthologies
Biblical books composed by the prophets are anthologies of various messages presented by a given biblical prophet during their ministry, unlike flowing narrative or legal requirements. Pericopes or paragraphs in prophetic books are rarely arranged in chronological order, nor do they always have a contextual flow (between pericopes) like one finds in narrative literature but are more often arranged according to the themes they address. Consequently, an interpreter of prophetic literature should not be surprised at the difficulty of outlining the messages of a prophetic book.

Foretelling or Forth-Telling?
The word "prophecy" generally signifies foretelling or predicting something that is going to happen in the future (foretelling). In reality, the Old Testament prophets spend much more time preaching ("telling forth") rather than predicting the future. The biblical prophets spend much more time addressing Israel's disobedience and the impending judgment the nation would face as a consequence of their rebellion.

The Message of the Prophets

As stated in the preceding section, the biblical prophets grounded their message in the Mosaic Covenant. Their message generally had three areas of emphasis: indictment and call to repentance, promise of judgment for rebellion, and the hope of ultimate restoration.

Indictment and Call to Repentance
The prophets emphasize the seriousness and extent of Israel's rebellion against Yahweh. Evidence of this rebellion falls into three categories: idolatry, social injustice, and religious ritualism. First of all, the idolatry practiced by Israel generally did not entail the absolute and total rejection of Yahweh but involved syncretism, combining worship of Yahweh with the worship of other so-called gods. Secondly, Yahweh demanded his chosen people to treat their fellow Israelites with justice and equity, esp. with regard to the weaker elements of Israelite society (e.g., aliens, widows, and orphans) (Deut. 10:17–19; 19:15–21; 24:17–22). Finally, God's people seemed to forget regularly that "ritual was the means to the relationship and not a substitute for the relationship" (Duvall and Hays, *Grasping God's Word*, 375). Yahweh rejected both Israel's sacrifices (Isa. 1:11–13) and fasting (Isa. 58:6–7) that were not offered from a genuinely obedient heart.

Promise of Judgment for Rebellion
These statements do not represent empty threats since they derive from the Deuteronomic expression of blessings and curses. The most serious consequence is expulsion from the land of promise.

Hope of Ultimate Restoration
This aspect of the prophetic messages is found in the messianic promises and future predictions made by the prophets. These marvelous promises center in the coming and work of the Messiah, Jesus Christ.

Basic Theme Statements
- **Isaiah.** The holy God will not permit unholiness in his people and will therefore chasten and purge them and make them fit to participate in his program of extending his rule over the Gentiles.
- **Jeremiah.** Jerusalem will fall if the people will not repent; nevertheless, God's rule is assured through a new covenant.
- **Lamentations.** A song lamenting the destruction of Jerusalem with hope for the future based on God's faithfulness.
- **Ezekiel.** From the time his presence departed from his covenant people until the consummation of his grand design for humanity God will carry out his saving purposes in the world.
- **Daniel.** The arrogant sovereignty of man, which

THE PROPHETS
and the kings who reigned during their lifetime

		Kings of Israel	Kings of Judah
8th century B.C. 799-700	Amos	Jeroboam II, Zachariah, Shallum, Menahem	Uzziah
	Hosea	Jeroboam II, Zachariah, Shallum, Menahem, Pekahiah, Pekah, Hoshea	Uzziah, Jotham, Ahaz, Hezekiah
	?Jonah	Jeroboam II	Uzziah
	Isaiah	Shallum, Menahem, Pekahiah, Pekah, Hoshea	Uzziah, Jotham, Ahaz, Hezekiah, Manasseh
	Micah	Pekahiah, Pekah, Hoshea End of the northern kingdom	Jotham, Ahaz, Hezekiah, Manasseh
7th century B.C. 699-600	Nahum		Josiah
	Zephaniah		Josiah
	Jeremiah		Josiah, Jehoahaz, Jehoiakim, Jehoiachin, Zedekiah
	Habakkuk		Josiah
6th century B.C. 599-500	Daniel		Jehoiakim, Jehoiachin, Zedekiah
	Ezekiel		Jehoiachin, Zedekiah
	Zechariah		Josiah
	Haggai		
	?Joel		
	?Obadiah		
5th century B.C. 499-400	Malachi		

?—some debate about the precise date

seeks to deny God, will be overturned so that God might reign.
- **Hosea.** In spite of Israel's unfaithfulness, Yahweh's faithful love will prevail.
- **Joel.** Divine judgment is to be visited upon Israel in the day of the Lord.
- **Amos.** The Lord is faithful to his covenant and to his law.
- **Obadiah.** The Lord will revenge Israel against Edom.
- **Jonah.** Jonah reminds Israel that she is a priestly nation and is to be God's tool of blessing the world.
- **Micah.** The Lord will judge the nations of the world (including Israel) and then form his purified people into a mighty nation under the rulership of the messianic king.
- **Nahum.** The sovereign Lord will avenge the harm done to his covenant people by judging the Assyrian oppressors.
- **Habakkuk.** The sovereign Lord will judge the injustice of Judah (through the Babylonians) and will sustain the faithful through the ordeal and eventually deliver Israel from foreign oppression.
- **Zephaniah.** In the Day of the Lord Yahweh will bring chastisement upon all the disobedient and enable a faithful remnant to populate the purified city and rejoice in the Lord's deliverance and protection.
- **Haggai.** The sovereign Lord promised to restore agricultural prosperity and assured his people that he would eventually overthrow the nations, glorify his temple, and bring honor to the Davidic dynasty.
- **Zechariah.** God will purify and restore Israel as his priestly nation in the glorious millennial state.
- **Malachi.** The Lord will come quickly with fire and with rewards to purify his theocracy.

I will raise up for them a prophet like you from among their brothers; I will put my words in his mouth, and he will tell them everything I command him.
Deuteronomy 18:18

Poetry and Wisdom Literature

The descriptive terms "poetic literature" and "wisdom literature" are overlapping but not synonymous expressions. Poetry comprises about one-third of the Hebrew Old Testament (sections in narrative literature, several prophetic books), with most of it found in Psalms, Proverbs, Song of Solomon, as well as much of Job and Ecclesiastes. Wisdom literature seeks to teach practical moral behavior or wrestle with significant problems related to human existence. It emphasizes the "life-focus" of certain biblical books (or sections of books—Job, Proverbs, Ecclesiastes, Song of Solomon, and wisdom psalms).

Poetic Literary Character
- *Poetic rhythm of thought.* The genius of Hebrew poetry involves thought rhyme, which concerns parallelism (the correspondence of one thought with another). Two common kinds of parallelism are synonymous (saying the same thing in both poetic lines in nearly the same way—Pss. 2:4; 3:1; 7:16) and synthetic (second line takes up and develops a thought begun in the first line—Pss. 1:1; 95:3). Other kinds of parallelism are emblematic (Pss. 23:1–2, 4; 57:1; 103:13; 113:5–6), antithetical (Pss. 1:6; 57:6), and inverted (Ps. 51:3; Isa. 11:13).
- *Poetic rhythm of sound (in Hebrew).* Similarity in sound served as a mnemonic tool as well as a means of emphasis. Acrostic Poems were written so that the initial letters of consecutive lines form an alphabet, word, or phrase

Replica of a *kinnor*, or lyre, which would have accompanied singing of the psalms.

Basic Theme Statements

- **Job.** The suffering believer must learn to live by faith in the sovereign creator and ruler of the cosmos, for his rule is righteous and wise.
- **Psalms.** As the Creator of the universe, God exercises sovereign authority over the natural order, the nations, and Israel, his servant nation. In his role as universal King, God promises to establish order and justice in the world and among his people, often by exhibiting his power as an invincible warrior. The only acceptable response to this sovereign King is trust and praise.
- **Proverbs.** A collection of maxims to give the student instruction in the skill of living a practical, righteous, and productive life.
- **Ecclesiastes.** In spite of the apparent futility involved in human existence, people should live life skillfully by trusting God's sovereignty, goodness, and justice.
- **Song of Solomon.** To extol human love and marriage.

(Pss. 9; 10; 25; 34; 37; 11; 112; 119; 145; Prov. 31:10–31; Lam. 1; 2; 3; 4; Nah. 1:2–20). Alliteration concerns the consonance of sounds at the beginning of words or syllables (Ps. 122:6). Assonance refers to vowels sounds, often at the end of words in order to emphasize an idea, theme, or tone (Ps. 119:29). Paronomasia describes word play through the repetition of words of similar sound, but not necessarily meaning in order to heighten the impact of the message (Gen. 32:22–24). Inclusio concerns the repetition of words or phrases by which the poet returns to the point from which he began (Ps. 118:1, 29).

Kinds of Psalms

- **Psalms of lament or complaint.** These comprise the largest group in the psalter. Some related to the entire nation and arose from times of national crisis (community laments—e.g., 44; 60; 74, et al.). Other psalms of this type relate to individual circumstances (individual laments—e.g., 3–7; 42–43; 51; 69; 70; 71, et al.). These psalms typically involve a complaint, a request for help, an affirmation of trust in God, and a vow to praise God when the crisis has passed.
- **Psalms of praise and thanksgiving.** The entire psalter depicts God as totally worthy of praise, but some psalms focus on that truth. Declarative praise of thanksgiving psalms of the individual offer praise or thanksgiving to God because of some kind of personal deliverance (Pss. 30; 32; 121, et al.). These psalms originated as a grateful response to God for a specific act of deliverance, such as healing from illness (chaps. 30; 32; 116), which may be a physical manifestation of unforgiven sin (chap. 32), or deliverance from enemies (chaps. 18; 92; 118; 138), or simply rescue from trouble (66:14). Descriptive praise psalms of the people affirm praise of God for his works among men (chaps. 24; 100; 113, et al.).
- **Wisdom Psalms.** These were related in their motifs with wisdom literature in the Hebrew Scriptures (e.g., Proverbs—e.g., Pss. 1; 37; 112; 127, et al.).
- **Pilgrim Psalms.** They all have the heading, "A song of ascents" which probably refer to Israel's "going up" to Jerusalem for the three festivals (Passover and Unleavened Bread, Weeks or Pentecost, Atonement and Tabernacles—Pss. 120–134).
- **Royal Psalms.** These emphasize the anointed King after the line of David (Pss. 2; 18; 21; 45; 72; 89; 101; 110; 132; 144).
- **Enthronement Psalms.** Songs of God's Kingship characterized by the expression "The Lord reigns" (Pss. 93; 96–97; 99), the Lord is "the great King" (Pss. 47; 95), or the Lord "comes to judge" (Ps. 98).

Jews visiting Jerusalem for the festivals would have this view from the Mount of Olives.

Religious Life

Worship in the Old Testament was not simply a matter of attending a service one or several times a week. Although certain activities and certain days for worship were prescribed in the Mosaic Law, worship affected every area of an Israelite's life. The Old Testament made no distinctions between secular and sacred realms of life. As people set apart by Yahweh's election of them, every part of life was to be carried out as an act of gratitude for all that God had done for his chosen people. Loving the Lord with their entire being (Deut. 6:5) meant that every Israelite was to wholeheartedly embrace this relationship with their God and devote every element of their being to living a life of absolute loyalty.

Although some might divide various Mosaic laws in logical or topical categories like moral, civil, and ceremonial, these categories are misleading. Genuine obedience to God's expectations in every area of life was moral as well as an act of worship. Also, the God of Israel

The young boy Samuel aids the High Priest Eli in the Temple at Shiloh.

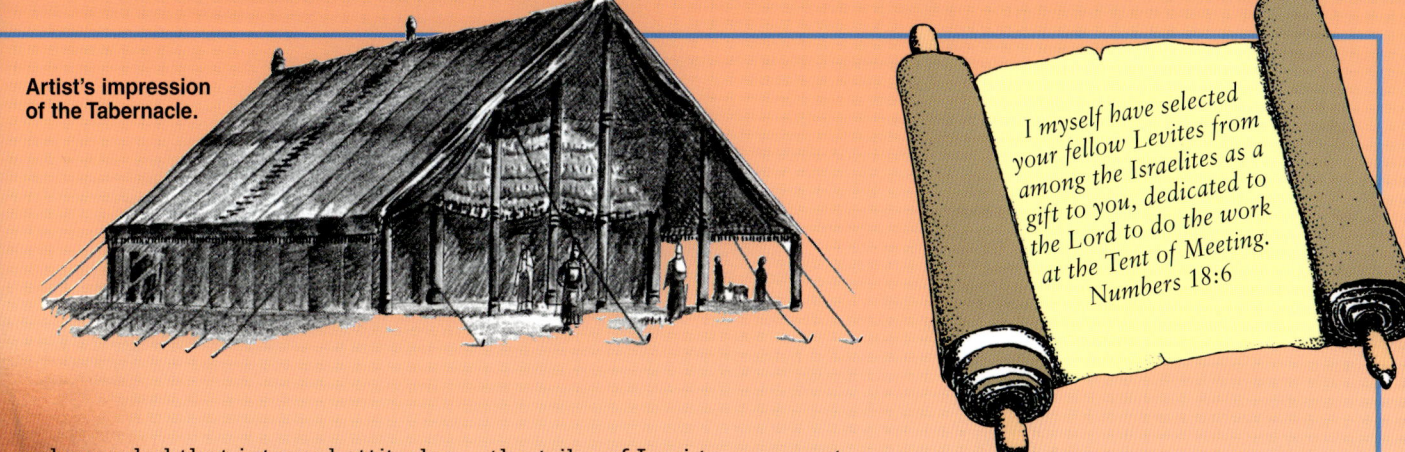

Artist's impression of the Tabernacle.

> I myself have selected your fellow Levites from among the Israelites as a gift to you, dedicated to the Lord to do the work at the Tent of Meeting.
> Numbers 18:6

demanded that internal attitudes as well as external conduct demonstrate his character to fellow Israelites as well as to the surrounding pagan nations.

Levites

Since the nation of Israel entered into a covenant relationship with a holy God, God demanded that they be holy as well (Lev. 20:7, 26). In order to provide people who could give direction to Israel's worship of Yahweh, the Lord set apart the tribe of Levi from the other eleven tribes for that purpose (Num. 1:47–51). That tribe received no tribal allotment but received several Levitical cities throughout the land of promise. They could have garden plots near those towns, but their main task was to facilitate local religious activities. During the wilderness wanderings they tore down, transported, and set up the tabernacle and all its related items (Num. 1:50–53). They also served as assistants for the priests (Num. 8:5–22). Moses and Aaron belonged to the tribe of Levi (Exod. 2:1–10; 4:14).

Priests

Although God commissioned the entire nation of Israel to function as a "kingdom of priests" (Exod. 19:6), he vested priestly functions in one tribe, the tribe of Levi. Aaron (Moses' brother) and his sons were selected out of the tribe of Levi to carry out priestly duties (Exod. 28–29). Every male child born to a priestly family would prepare for the priesthood from childhood, but had to meet certain qualifications to serve as a priest (Lev. 21:16–23). According to the book of Deuteronomy, the priests had several responsibilities, including using Urim and Thummim to obtain an oracle about various matters (17:9, 12; 19:17; 20:2; 21:5; 24:8); expounding the law of Moses (17:18; 27:9–10; 31:9–11, 24–26), serving before the ark (10:7–8; 31:9, 25), and sacrificing and receiving offerings (18:1, 3; 26:4). They would ensure that Israelite worshipers brought appropriate

High Priest in his ceremonial costume.

sacrifices and would carry out the actual sacrifice. Because there were more priests than needed for temple ministry, other priests lived in the Levitical cities throughout the land and taught the Law to God's people.

High Priest

One Levitical priest was appointed to serve as Israel's High Priest. This priest had to match a unique set of requirements (Lev. 21:10–15). He would wear special clothing, including a gold breastplate inlaid with twelve precious stones representing each tribe of Israel (Exod. 28). Once each year, on the Day of Atonement, he would enter the Holy of Holies alone and sprinkle blood from specified sacrifices to consecrate that part of the tabernacle (Lev. 16:3–19). Whenever a high priest died, any Israelites who had found shelter in a City of Refuge because they committed accidental murder was able to return to their home without fear of reprisal (Num. 35:28).

Miscellaneous Temple servants

Throughout Israel's history, various individuals from different tribes served at the tabernacle or temple as musicians as part of the nation's worship of their God as well as craftsmen, gold and silver workers, needleworkers, and others who helped design and construct the tabernacle and temple (Exod. 31:1–11; 35:30–39:43).

Religious Buildings

At the heart of the Mosaic Covenant is the affirmation "I will be your God and you will be my people," based on numerous occurrences of the expressions "the Lord your God" and "my people." The nation of Israel entered into a covenant relationship with the Lord (Exod. 19), and the Lord demanded that his people worship him exclusively. In the book of Exodus, the Lord revealed to Moses detailed instructions for building a place of worship for the Israelites, the tabernacle (Exod. 25–27; 30:1–10, 17–21). Later God revealed to David and Solomon the plan for a more permanent structure, the temple (1 Kings 5–6; 1 Chron. 28:11–19). Unlike modern churches, both of these structures were not places for God's people to hear the preaching and teaching of God's Word. On the one hand, these holy structures provided a means for a holy God to dwell in the midst of a sinful people. The visible presence of God (Shechinah glory) rose above the Ark of the Covenant in the Holy of Holies (see below) as a reminder that the Israelites had entered into a covenant relationship with this great God. Its location provided a barrier between a holy God and his sinful people. On the other hand, both of these structures served as the primary place for God's people to maintain their relationship with their God (through various sacrifices—see next section).

Tabernacle

This structure, also called the "tent of meeting" (Exod. 33:7), was erected to facilitate Israel's worship of Yahweh until a permanent structure could be built. The entire structure was 100 cubits long and 50 cubits wide (150 ft. by 75 ft.). When God indicated that it was time for the Israelites to continue their journey, the Levites would tear it down, transport all the parts, and erect it in the new encampment. Unlike the temple, the tabernacle was surrounded by white linen curtains and four cloth/skin layers covered the central structure (Holy Place and Holy of Holies). Otherwise, the layout of the tabernacle was similar to that of the temple (see comments below).

Temple

Although David asked if he could build the temple, God gave that privilege to his son, Solomon. David prepared for its construction by gathering an abundance of materials (1 Chron. 29:1–9). Solomon's temple was made out of stone, was larger than the tabernacle (over twice as large), and was surrounded by a large courtyard.

Courtyard

A courtyard surrounded the primary structure containing the Holy Place and the Holy of Holies. Since that structure was at the back center of the Courtyard, most activity took place in the front half, where the bronze laver and altar were located.

- *Bronze Laver.* After entering the courtyard, the priests were required to wash their hands and feet in the water of this laver before they offered any sacrifices (Exod. 30:17–21). The laver of the Solomonic temple was 15 feet in diameter.

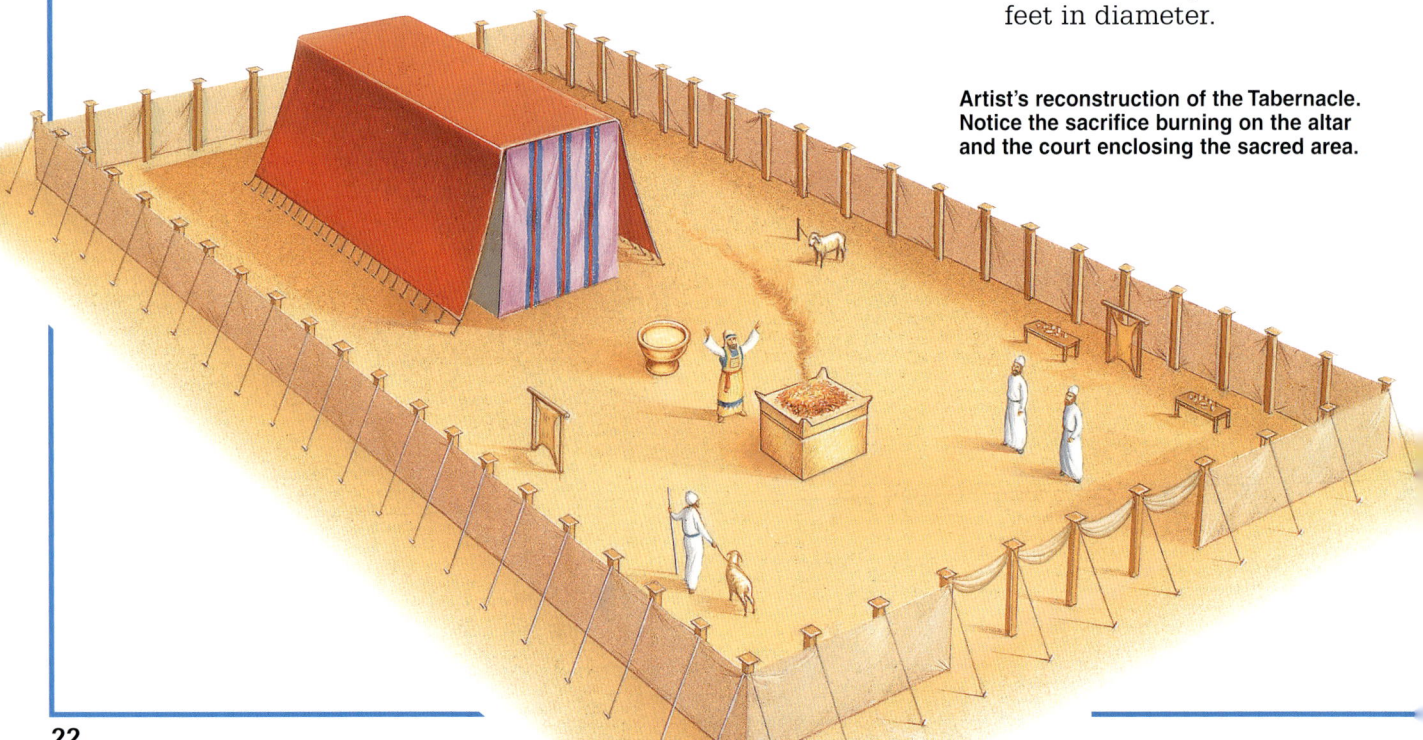

Artist's reconstruction of the Tabernacle. Notice the sacrifice burning on the altar and the court enclosing the sacred area.

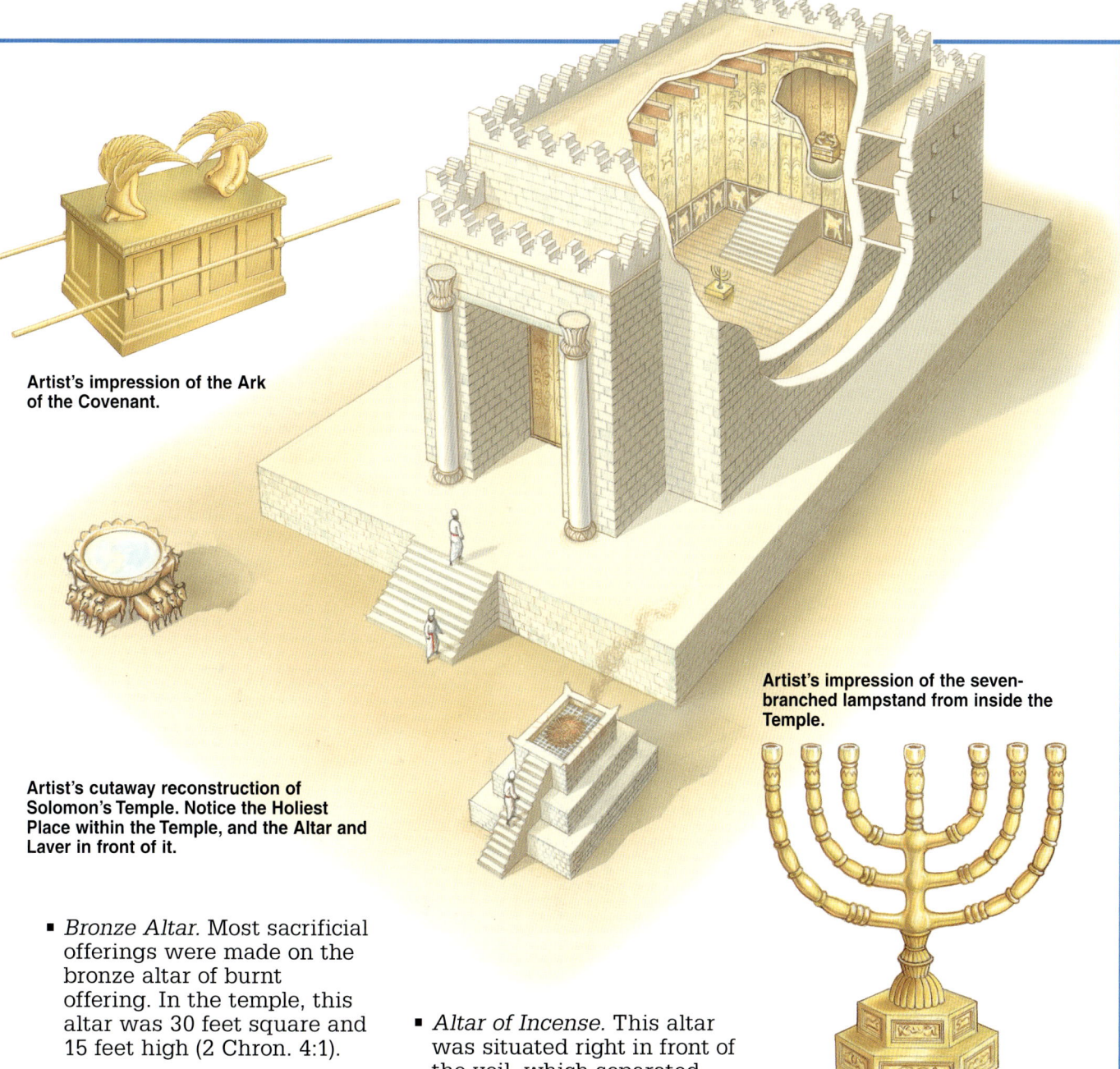

Artist's impression of the Ark of the Covenant.

Artist's cutaway reconstruction of Solomon's Temple. Notice the Holiest Place within the Temple, and the Altar and Laver in front of it.

Artist's impression of the seven-branched lampstand from inside the Temple.

- *Bronze Altar.* Most sacrificial offerings were made on the bronze altar of burnt offering. In the temple, this altar was 30 feet square and 15 feet high (2 Chron. 4:1).

Holy Place

The structure within the courtyard had two sections. The front section, the Holy Place, contained three key items.

- *Table of Showbread.* This table (Exod. 25:25–30) was located on the right (north) side of the Holy Place. The priests would place twelve fresh loaves of unleavened bread on this table on every Sabbath (one for each Israelite tribe—Lev. 24:5–9).
- *Golden Lampstand.* This lampstand was located on the left (south) side and was always lit, providing light for this room (Exod. 25:31–39).
- *Altar of Incense.* This altar was situated right in front of the veil, which separated the Holy Place from the Holy of Holies (Exod. 30:1–10). The priest had to burn incense at this altar in the morning and at twilight (Exodus 30:7–8), as a perpetual fragrance before the Lord.

Holy of Holies

The High Priest would enter this rear room only once each year (on the Day of Atonement).

- *Veil.* A multicolored curtain served as the barrier that kept the priests from looking into or entering the Holy of Holies (Exod. 26:31–37).
- *Ark of the Covenant.* This wooden box (ca. 3.75 ft. by 2.25 by 2.25 ft.) was the only furniture item in the Holy of Holies (Exod. 25:10–22). It contained the Ten Commandments (2 Kings 11:12), the pot of manna (Exod. 16:33–35), and Aaron's rod that budded (Num. 17:10). Two figures of golden angels were situated on the top of the Ark, facing each other with their wings touching (called the mercy seat—Exod. 25:17–22). The divine presence rested between these two angels.

Religious Activity

Israel's religious activity must be understood against backdrop the nation's covenant relationship with Yahweh. In normal political/covenantal relationships, a vassal or subordinate ruler would occasionally offend his suzerain and need to sue for peace and the normalization of relationships. The suzerain or superior ruler would also expect regular re-affirmations of loyalty, expressed by periodic appearances at the palace. Against that backdrop, the sacrifices Yahweh demanded of Israel would have demonstrated the willing submission of Israel to Yahweh's rule as well as atoned for her offenses against her sovereign, Yahweh.

These sacrifices (and feast days and tithes) must also be understood in light of holiness. In Exodus 25–40 God gave all the instructions for the building of the tabernacle. The climax of the section comes in 40:34–38 when the Shechinah Glory (God's presence manifested in a cloud) swept into residence. Since God himself dwells in the midst of his chosen people, how should his chosen people live? By offering the required sacrifices, give special focus on certain feasts, and give back to Yahweh a portion of what He has given them. These all serve as a kind of tribute offered by the Israelites (the vassal) to their great God (the suzerain).

Sacrificial System

Yahweh originally established a covenant relationship with Abraham and his descendants in Genesis 12. As Abraham had done (Gen. 15:6), his descendants were able to enjoy a relationship with Yahweh through faith. Through Moses, several centuries later, the Lord required that his covenant nation offer certain sacrifices to him. As with Abraham, salvation was by faith and not works. These sacrifices had nothing to do with a person beginning their relationship with God and everything to do with maintaining that relationship with God. There were two broad categories of sacrifices.

1. *Voluntary act of worship.* For the burnt offering (Lev. 1; 6:8–13, et al.), the entire bull, ram, or male bird was consumed on the altar to express the devotion of the worshipper (or atonement for unintentional sin). A token portion of unleavened cakes or grains was offered as a meal or grain offering as an act of worship (Lev. 2; 6:14–23). Any animal from the herds of flocks (without blemish) could be offered as a peace or fellowship offering (Lev. 3; 7:11–34). Only the fat portion of the animal would be burned and the rest would be shared in a fellowship meal by the priest and the offerer's family.

2. *Mandatory atonement for sin.* The sin and guilt offerings overlap, but seem to have a distinct identity. Depending on the circumstances, a young bull, male or female goat or lamb, a dove or pigeon, or a prescribed portion of flour would be offered as part of a sin offering (Lev. 4), and the priests were allowed to eat all but the fat portions. The guilt offering involved an unblemished ram and the priests were able to eat all but the fat portions (Lev. 5:1–6:7). The sin offering appears to have dealt with guilt for some purification offense where there could be no restitution. The guilt offering took place when restitution was possible.

Feast Calendar

Three of the feasts (see chart) represented part of the homage

Sacrifice at the altar before the Tabernacle.

The Jewish Calendar

The Jewish calendar was ordered both by the movements of the sun, moon, and stars, and also by the national festivals and the agricultural cycle.

The year was divided into months marked by the phases of the moon, with an extra month added every few years to adjust as necessary.

#	Months	Season	Months	#	Festivals
1	JANUARY	Winter	SHEBAT	11	
2	FEBRUARY		ADAR	12	Purim
3	MARCH	Spring	NISAN	1	Passover and Unleavened Bread
4	APRIL		IYYAR	2	
5	MAY		SIVAN	3	Harvest/Weeks (Pentecost)
6	JUNE	Summer	TAMMUZ	4	
7	JULY		AB	5	
8	AUGUST		ELUL	6	
9	SEPTEMBER		TISHRI	7	Trumpets (New Year) Tabernacles/Shelters
10	OCTOBER		MARCHESVAN	8	
11	NOVEMBER		KISLEV	9	Lights (Temple dedication)
12	DECEMBER	Winter	TEBETH	10	

due Yahweh: Passover (and Unleavened Bread), Feast of Weeks, and Feast of Tabernacle (cf. Exod. 23:14–18; 34:18–26; Lev. 23; Deut. 16:1–17). They formed part of the "sacred rhythm" of Israel's life. The first two feasts framed the spring grain harvest, while the Feast of Tabernacles occurred in the fall when the new grain and wine are stored away for the winter. All three commemorated God's deliverance of his people through the Exodus from Egypt and expressed gratitude for the harvest. For these three feasts, all Israelite men were to make the pilgrimage to the central sanctuary to appear before the Yahweh, the great King. This "national" gathering of Israelites from all parts of the land of promise would remind them of their national identity as God's covenant people.

Sabbath

In Exodus 20:8–11 and Deuteronomy 5:12–15 the Lord requires the Israelites to set aside the seventh day of the week for special purposes. Unlike an ordinary day of work, the Sabbath was to be set aside for a special function, to celebrate God's activity on behalf of his people. All people (both free and enslaved) and all animals normally used for work are to enjoy this Sabbath rest. No one and no animal was supposed to work on this special day. The Sabbath day was not simply intended as a day of inactivity, but also as a day of celebration. God's people were to take this opportunity to celebrate God's purposes demonstrated in his creative and redemptive work.

Tithes and Offerings

Building on other tithing passages (Gen 14:20; 28:22;), Moses commanded the children of Israel to set aside one-tenth of their produce (grain, new wine, and oil) and the firstborn of their herds and flocks each year and devote them to the Lord (Lev 27:30–32; Num 18:21–28; Deut. 14:21–29). The pedagogical purpose for this practice was to teach God's chosen people to fear him always (cf. 4:10; 17:19). Their prosperity did not result from their irrigation or advanced agricultural techniques, but was

A rabbi holds the Torah aloft in a synagogue.

due to Yahweh's fixed commitment to his covenant promises. In addition to tithing, Yahweh encouraged Israelites to give generously on other occasions as well.

Old Testament Covenants

Old Testament covenants played a prominent role in social, political, and religious life. Although the Hebrew word for "covenant" (*berît*) can have different meanings, when used with reference to biblical covenants, it highlighted two basic nuances. In the first place, it signified a legally binding obligation. A covenant was never something into which a person would lightly enter. Secondly, a covenant did not represent an arbitrary dumping of expectations on an unsuspecting recipient, but assumed the existence of a pre-existing relationship. The Noahic, Abrahamic, Davidic, and new covenants are often called "covenants of promise" or *grant* covenants, whereas the Mosaic covenant is likened to a "suzerain-vassal" *treaty* (see text box for a delineation of some of the fundamental differences between these two types of covenants).

Noahic Covenant (Grant)

Although this covenant was made with Noah (and his descendants—Gen. 9:8–10), it encompassed all of humanity since Noah and his family were the only survivors of the flood. God unilaterally promised that He would never destroy all life on earth through some natural catastrophe (Gen. 9:11). He designated the rainbow as a sign of the covenant, a repeated memorial to remind mankind of God's gracious promise.

The Abrahamic Covenant (Grant)

The Abrahamic Covenant is a personal and family covenant that forms the historical foundation for God's dealings with mankind. Through this covenant God promises Abraham and his descendants land, seed, and blessing (Gen. 12:1–3). The Abrahamic covenant delineates the unique role that Abraham's seed will have in God's plan for the world and paves the way for Israel's prominent role in that plan.

The Mosaic Covenant (Treaty)

This covenant follows the format of a bilateral suzerain-vassal treaty and represents the constitution for the nation of Israel that grew out of the Abraham's descendants, a development envisioned by the Abrahamic covenant. In this covenant God offered cursing for disobedience and blessing for obedience. God's basic demand was that Israel would love him exclusively (Deut. 6:4–5). This covenant gave God's chosen people with tangible guidelines to enable them to demonstrate the character of Yahweh before the surrounding nations (Exod. 19:4–6).

The Davidic Covenant (Grant)

Yahweh unilaterally promised to establish and maintain the Davidic dynasty on the throne of Israel (2 Sam. 7:12–16). This covenant finds its ultimate fulfillment when Christ returns to rule over believing Israel during the millennium. Theologically, this covenant is rooted in the Abrahamic covenant. Regardless of whether a given generation (or generations) of Israelites experience divine judgment (in light of the blessings and cursings of the Mosaic Covenant), the Davidic dynasty would remain intact forever. God promised that Abraham's descendants would become a great nation with a land, ruled over by kings (Gen. 17). The Davidic Covenant further specifies that reality. The Davidic Covenant also relates to the Mosaic Covenant. The royal psalms depict the king as

Basic Differences Between a Grant and a Treaty

Grant
1. The giver of the covenant makes a commitment to the vassal.
2. Represents an obligation of the master to his vassal.
3. Primarily protects the rights of the vassal
4. No demands made by the superior party.

Treaty
1. The giver of the covenant imposes an obligation on the vassal.
2. Represents an obligation of the vassal to his master.
3. Primarily protects the rights of the vassal master.
4. The master promises to reward or punish the vassal for obeying or disobeying the imposed obligations.

Now if you obey me fully and keep my covenant, then out of all nations you will be my treasured possession.
Exodus 19:5

conducting his rule in accordance with the stipulations of the Mosaic covenant (Pss. 2; 18; 21; 45; 72; 89; 101; 110; 132; 144; cf. 2 Kings 18:6; 21:7–9; 23:24–25).

The New Covenant (Grant)
In this covenant the Lord promises to maintain his relationship with his chosen people in a different way than had characterized the Old Covenant, i.e., the Mosaic Covenant (Jer. 31:31–34). Among other things, he would write his law on their hearts and forgive their sins.

It is essential to observe a key difference between the *nature* of the Mosaic Covenant and the New Covenant. Since the Mosaic Covenant included believing and unbelieving Israelites, participating in that covenant did not *necessarily* include an internal conformity to Yahweh's requirements. What is fundamentally new in the New Covenant is that *every* participant in that covenant (unlike the Mosaic Covenant) receives this "new heart." Although *Judah's sin* was written on the heart of God's chosen nation in general under the Mosaic Covenant (Jer. 17:1), *God's law* will be written on the heart of every Israelite in that New Covenant setting.

Unlike the Mosaic Covenant, which was fallible (i.e., Israel could break that covenant), participants in the New Covenant cannot violate or breach the new arrangement. The New Covenant does not have a "built-in" fallibility because, unlike the Old Covenant, only believers are able to participate in the New Covenant. Whereas *only Yahweh* remained faithful to his commitments in the Mosaic covenant, *both partners* will live in accordance with the blessings and demands of the New Covenant (i.e., be loyal).

Conditional or Unconditional Covenants
When dealing with the biblical covenants, the concepts of conditionality and unconditionality are not mutually exclusive. An unconditional covenant is not necessarily without conditions just as a conditional covenant can have unconditional elements. The use of terms grant and treaty (see text box) clarifies the differences between the biblical covenants. In a *grant* the giver/maker of the covenant offers the promise or commitment (*unilateral*). It may be called unconditional in the sense that no demands are made on the superior party. In a *treaty* the giver/maker of the covenant imposes an obligation upon someone else (*bilateral*).

27

The God of the Old Testament
Who Was He?

The Old Testament is not primarily about the nation of Israel, great leaders, faith, or failure. Rather, it provides a vivid and clear revelation of God, a presentation that is filled out in the New Testament. Theological statements about God as well as narrative descriptions of his activity enable readers of the Old Testament to learn about the character of the God of Gods.

His Attributes and Character

- **Holy.** The basic idea of holiness is "apartness." Since God is totally separate from anything sinful, he is morally pure. He is also distinct from all that is common, making him absolutely unique or incomparable. The Old Testament regularly affirms that there is no God but him (Deut. 4:35, 39). Because he is holy, his chosen people must also be holy (Lev. 19:2).
- **Eternal.** The psalmist wrote: "Before the mountains were born or you brought forth the earth and the world, from everlasting to everlasting you are God" (Ps. 90:2). God is limitless as it relates to time.
- **Omnipresent.** When Solomon was dedicating the Temple, the place of Yahweh's residence on earth, he declared: "The heavens, even the highest heaven, cannot contain you. How much less this temple I have built!" No one can escape God's presence (Ps. 139:7–12).
- **Omnipotent.** God is able to do all things that conform to his perfect character. The prophet Jeremiah wrote: "Sovereign Lord, you have made the heavens and the earth by your great power and outstretched arm. Nothing is too hard for you" (Jer. 32:17). As the omnipotent God, he exercises absolute *sovereignty* over the entire creation. His will is decisive everywhere and always (Dan. 4:35).
- **Omniscient.** God knows all things actual and possible, past, present, and future, in one eternal act. He is not simply aware of what is happening in his creation, but is presented in the Old Testament as the God who predicts and brings to pass events. According to the psalmist, "Before a word is on my tongue you know it completely, O Lord" (Ps. 139:4; cf. 147:4).
- **Gracious.** As a gracious God, He gives what is absolutely undeserved to those who deserve nothing but evil (Jonah 4:2).
- **Faithful/Loyal.** The Hebrew word *chesed* provides a rich and vibrant description of God. Although translated in different ways (lovingkindness, loyal love, covenant love, faithfulness, etc.), it highlights a central truth. The God of the Old Testament is absolutely reliable, he remains firmly committed to whatever he has promised. The psalmist could cry out in confidence: "Deliver me because of your faithfulness!" (Ps. 6:4).
- **Loving.** Although this term includes an emotional aspect, throughout the Old Testament when it occurs in the context of the divine—human relationship, it seems to indicate a choice that manifests itself in a certain conduct. For God, to love is to choose (Mal. 1:2–3) and that love demonstrates itself in tangible provision of abundant blessings (Deut. 5:10).
- **Righteous and Just.** Righteousness can signify what one is, what they do, or what they declare others to be. Whenever it refers to behavior (whether human or divine), it clearly implies conduct that is measured in accordance with

And the glory of the Lord will be revealed, and all mankind together will see it.
Isaiah 40:5

Some Old Testament Name/Titles for God

Ancient of Days
(Dan. 7:9)

Creator
(Isaiah 40:28)

The Eternal God
(Gen. 16:13; 21:33)

Father
(Ps. 103:13; Jer. 3:19; 31:9)

Fear
(Gen. 31:42, 53)

God Almighty
(Gen. 17:1; Exod. 6:31; Ps. 91:1–2)

The God who sees
(Gen. 16:13)

The God of all mankind
(Jer. 32:27)

The God of the covenant
(Judg. 9:46)

The God of heaven
(Neh. 2:4)

The God of Israel
(Gen. 33:20; Pss. 68:8; 106:48)

Holy One
(Job 6:10)

Holy One of Israel
(Isa. 1:14; 5:19)

King
(Jer. 10:7)

The Living God
(Deut. 5:26)

The Lord/Adonai
(Pss. 2:4; 8:1; Isa. 40:3–5; Hab. 3:19)

The Lord/ Yahweh
(Exod. 3:14; 33:19)

The Lord will provide
(Gen. 22:13–14)

The Lord is my Banner
(Exod. 17:15)

The Lord that Heals
(Exod. 15:26)

The Lord is Peace
(Judg. 6:24)

The Lord my Shepherd
(Ps. 23:1)

The Lord our Righteousness
(Jer. 23:6)

The Lord of Hosts
(1 Sam. 1:11; 17:45)

The Lord is present/there
(Ezek. 48:35)

The Lord Most High
(Ps. 97:9)

The Lord that sanctifies You
(Exod. 31:13)

Mighty One
(Gen. 49:24; Ps. 132:25; Isa. 49:26)

The Most High God
(Gen. 14:19; Ps. 9:2)

Rock
(Deut. 32:4, 15, 18, 30–31)

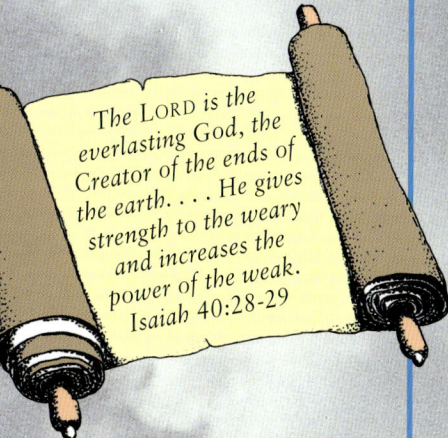

The Lord is the everlasting God, the Creator of the ends of the earth.... He gives strength to the weary and increases the power of the weak.
Isaiah 40:28-29

God acted out on the pages of history a clear picture of redemption from sin (something that the New Testament clearly develops further). Through his redemption of his chosen people, he demonstrates his absolute sovereignty over all nations and furthers his intention to form Israel into a nation that will serve as his channel for the ongoing work of redemption to the world (Isa. 45:22–23).

- **Warrior.** In addition to being Israel's deliver, the Lord serves as the One who fights for his covenant people (Exod. 15:3), whether it be against the Canaanites (Deut. 9:1–3) or any attacking army (Judg. 5:19–20), granting them victory against all odds.
- **Prosecutor and Judge.** Even though Yahweh chose Israel to serve as his covenant nation, if they choose to rebel against him, they will have to give an account to their God in his role of prosecutor and judge (Deut. 1:17). He will firmly punish their rebellion (Deut. 6:15; 7:4) and evict them from the land of promise (Deut. 4:27; 28:20–68).
- **King.** Although God includes human kings as part of his plan for the nation of Israel (Gen. 17; Deut. 17), he is "king" of the world, the gods, the nations, and Israel. In particular, the psalms depict Yahweh as the universal King who maintains order and justice in the world and before whom his subjects should respond with trust and praise. As the psalmist wrote: "The Lord has established his throne in heaven, and his kingdom rules over all."

some standard (Ps. 119:137). Justice is not merely a legal term, but signifies conduct that is characterized by equity or justice (Deut. 10:18).
- **Jealous.** As the One who has entered into an intimate covenant relationship with the nation of Israel, God refuses to share the love and worship of his covenant nation with other gods (Deut. 5:9). In other nations from that region, there is no expression of a god's envy or zeal in relation to a worshiper. In clear contrast to that reality, Yahweh tolerates no rivals. He demands the exclusive worship of his chosen people (Deut. 6:4).

His Function
- **Creator.** In addition to the fact that He brought the entire universe into existence (see next section), numerous passages refer to God as the creator of the universe (Gen. 1:1–2:3; Ps. 104:7–9) as well as the creator of the nation of Israel (Isa. 43:1). As the Creator, he can exercise sovereignty over his creation (Isa. 40:26, 28; 41:20; et al.).
- **Redeemer.** As the One who redeemed/delivered his covenant nation out of bondage in Egypt (Deut. 5:6, 16; 6:12, 21–23; 7:8),

The God of the Old Testament

What Did He Do and What Did He Demand?

Throughout the Old Testament, God revealed himself to his people, not only through indications of his flawless character (see previous section), but also through his activity on behalf of his creation (and his chosen people in particular). An understanding of the below events should be correlated with God's establishment of various covenants with the descendants of Abraham (see sections titled "From a People to a Nation" and "Old Testament Covenants").

What He Does

- **Creation.** Genesis 1–2 records God creating the world in six days. During the first three days of Creation, starting with a dark, water-covered globe, God brought into existence light, a distinct atmosphere, and a vegetated land mass surrounded by an ocean. During the last three days of Creation he filled that world with flying creatures in the sky, sea creatures in the water, and various land animals. His creation of Adam and Eve brought his creative work to completion.
- **Flood.** After Adam and Eve fell into sin (Gen. 3), humanity became so devoted to sin that God decided to purify the world through a severe judgment, a universal flood (Gen. 6–8). Only Noah, his three sons, and their wives (8 people) survived this terrible punishment. They served as the beginning of a new human population on earth.
- **Babel.** Because of the arrogance of Noah's descendants and to force them to spread out throughout the world, God confused their language so various groups of people spoke different languages (Gen. 11:1–9). After finding people who spoke a common language, groups of people headed in different directions to set up new living centers.
- **Exodus.** After entering into a special covenant relationship with Abraham (see section on Old Testament covenants) and through a famine in Canaan, God caused Jacob and his descendants ("Hebrews") to move from Canaan to Egypt. A few centuries later, the Egyptians made the Hebrews their slaves. God raised up Moses to deliver his elect people out of Egypt and to lead them to the land of promise (Exod. 2). After an extended time away from Egypt, God directed Moses to return and demand that the Pharaoh release the Israelites. The Pharaoh refused to do this until after Ten Plagues, which left the land of Egypt devastated.

- **Conquest.** Forty years after leaving Egypt, the Israelites crossed the Jordan River and entered the land of Canaan, a land God promised his chosen nation. The conquest of Canaan brought to initial fulfillment God's promise to Abraham that he would give them a land (Gen. 12:1) and make them a great people (Deut. 10:22).
- **Judgment/Exile.** In light of his demand that the nation of Israel wholeheartedly obey his covenant demands (Mosaic Covenant), God addressed Israel's rebellion against that covenant with judgment, often at the hands of powerful Gentile nations. Eventually, because of their penchant for rebellion, God allowed the Assyrians and the Babylonians to conquer Israel and Judah (722 B.C. and 586 B.C. respectively). A disruption in Israel's relationship with their *covenant lord* occasioned a disruption in their enjoyment of the *covenant land*. After Cyrus' defeat of Babylon in 539 B.C., a number of Israelites returned to their homeland (Ezra–Nehemiah). The consummation of God's intentions for the nation of Israel will occur after Jesus Christ returns to earth for the second time.

What He Demands
- **Genesis 1:26–28.** In addition to creating mankind in accordance to his image, he made man and woman to serve as his image-bearers. They were to extend his rule over all creation. Adam and Eve's fall into sin interrupted the accomplishment of that plan, but did not preclude it.
- **Genesis 12.** As a way of carrying out his plan to extend his rule over all creation, God chose Abraham to father a people who would serve as his servant nation, a conduit of God's blessing for the rest of the world.
- **Exodus 19:4–6.** Right before God established the Mosaic Covenant with Israel, he delineated his intended rationale for that covenant. By genuinely living in accordance to his covenantal demands, the nation of Israel would be able to serve as a witness nation before the pagan nations. In other words, by living out God's character before the surrounding nations, they could have a powerful impact on that world.

He tends his flock like a shepherd: He gathers the lambs in his arms . . .
Isaiah 40:11

Index

Abraham, 3, 4, 5, 7, 24, 26, 30, 31
Adam, 3, 4, 30, 31
allegiance, 13, 15
alliance, 7, 9
altar, 22, 23, 24
Ark of the Covenant, 22, 23
atonement, 19, 21, 23, 24

Babylon, 10, 11, 17, 31
blessings/curses, 16, 26, 27, 28

Canaan, 4, 5, 7, 8, 29, 30, 31
conditional, 27
Conquest, 7, 31
Covenant, 7, 10, 12–17, 21, 22, 24, 25, 26–27, 28, 29, 30, 31
Creation, 3, 4, 28, 29, 30, 31
curses. See blessings

David, 8–9, 10, 19, 22, 26
Day of Atonement, 21, 23

Eden, Garden of, 4

Egypt, 4, 6–7, 9, 12, 13, 25, 29, 30, 31
Eve, 4, 30
exile, 10, 31
Exodus, 6, 7, 13, 25

feasts/festivals, 19, 24, 25
Flood, 4, 26, 30

grant, 26–27

High Priest, 20, 21, 23
holiness, 24, 28

idolatry, 8, 9, 16
injustice, 16, 17
Isaac, 4
Isaiah, 10, 14, 16, 17
Israel, 3, 7, 8–9, 10–11, 12, 14, 15, 16–17, 19, 20, 21, 22, 24, 25, 26, 27, 28, 29, 31

Jacob, 4, 6, 30
Jerusalem, 8, 10, 11, 16, 19
Joseph, 4, 6

Joshua, 7, 8, 9, 11
Judah. 8, 9, 10, 16, 17, 31
judge, 8, 17, 29

king, 8, 10, 17, 19, 25, 26–27, 29

Law, 7, 12–13, 14, 17, 20, 21, 27
Levites, 21, 22

Noah, 4, 26, 30
Northern Kingdom, 10, 17

offering, 23, 24

Passover, 7, 19, 25
Persia, 11
poetry/poetic literature, 14, 18
Priests, 10, 13, 15, 21, 22, 23, 24
Promised Land, 5, 7
Proverbs, 9, 18, 19
prophets/prophecy, 10, 14–15, 16
Psalms, 8, 9, 14, 18, 19, 26, 29

rebellion, 4, 7, 8, 10, 14, 15, 16
redemption, 29

relationship, 16, 20, 21, 22
Return, 10–11
ritualism, 16

Sabbath, 13, 23, 25
sacrifice, 21, 22, 24
Saul, 8, 9
Shechinah glory, 22, 24
Sinai, 7, 12, 13, 14
Sojourn, 6, 7, 13
Solomon, 9, 18, 22, 28
Southern Kingdom, 10
suzerain, 24, 26

Tabernacle, 21–22, 24, 25
Temple, 9, 11, 17, 21, 22, 23, 25, 28
Ten Commandments, 12–13, 23
Theocratic anointing, 8, 9
tithes, 24, 25
treaty, 12, 26, 27

unconditional, 27
Ur, 4, 5

vassal, 24, 26, 27

wilderness, 6, 7, 21
Wisdom literature, 18, 19
worship, 13, 16, 20, 21, 22, 24, 29

For Further Reading

General
Dyer, C., and E. Merrill. *Nelson's Old Testament Survey*. Nashville: Thomas Nelson, 2001.
Duvall, J., and D. Hays. *Grasping God's Word: A Hands-on Approach to Reading, Interpreting, and Applying the Bible*. Grand Rapids: Zondervan, 2005.
Merrill, E. *Everlasting Dominion: A Theology of the Old Testament*. Nashville: Broadman & Holman, 2006.
———. *Kingdom of Priests: A History of Old Testament Israel*. Grand Rapids: Baker, 1987.
Merrill, E., M. Rooker, and M. Grisanti. *Old Testament Introduction*. Nashville: Broadman & Holman, forthcoming.
Rose Book of Bible Charts, Maps, and Time Lines. Torrance, CA: Rose, 2005.
Walton, J., and A. Hill. *Old Testament Today*. Grand Rapids: Zondervan, 2004.
Zuck, R., ed. *A Biblical Theology of the Old Testament*. Chicago: Moody, 1991.

Commentaries
Gaebelein, F. *Expositor's Bible Commentary*. Grand Rapids: Zondervan, 1976–1988. A revised edition is forthcoming, edited by T. Longman III and D. Garland. There are numerous Old Testament commentaries available, but the reader will do well to begin with the *Expositor's Bible Commentary*.

Genesis–Deuteronomy
Ashley, T. *The Book of Numbers*. Grand Rapids: Eerdmans, 1993.
Currid, J. *Exodus*. Auburn, MA: Evangelical Press, 2000–2001.
Hamilton, V. *Handbook on the Pentateuch*. Grand Rapids: Baker, 2005.
Merrill, E. *Deuteronomy*. Nashville: Broadman & Holman, 1994.
Rooker, M. *Leviticus*. Nashville: Broadman & Holman, 2000.
Ross, A. *Creation and Blessing: A Guide to the Study and Exposition of Genesis*. Grand Rapids: Baker, 1988.

Joshua–Esther
Duguid, I. *Esther and Ruth*. Phillipsburg, NJ: P & R, 2005.
Hamilton, V. *Handbook on the Historical Books*. Grand Rapids: Baker, 2001.
Provan, I. *1–2 Kings*. Peabody, MA: Hendrickson, 1995.
Smith, J. *1–2 Samuel*. Joplin, MO: College Press, 2000.
Thompson, J. *1, 2 Chronicles*. Nashville: Broadman & Holman, 1994.

Poetic/Wisdom Literature
Estes, D. *Handbook on the Wisdom Books and Psalms*. Grand Rapids: Baker, 2005.
Garrett, D. *Proverbs, Ecclesiastes, Song of Songs*. Nashville: Broadman & Holman, 1993.
Mayhue, R. *Practicing Proverbs*. Great Britain: Christian Focus, 2003.
Wilson, G. *Psalms*. Grand Rapids: Zondervan, 2002.

Prophetic Literature
Allen, L. *The Books of Joel, Obadiah, Jonah, and Micah*. Grand Rapids: Eerdmans, 1976.
Busenitz, I. *Joel and Obadiah*. Great Britain: Christian Focus, 2003.
Chisholm, R., Jr. *Interpreting the Minor Prophets*. Grand Rapids: Zondervan, 1990.
Finley, T. *Joel, Amos, Obadiah*. http://www.bible.org.
Merrill, E. *Haggai, Zechariah, Malachi*. http://www.bible.org.
Miller, S. *Daniel*. Nashville: Broadman & Holman, 1994.
Oswalt, J. *Isaiah*. Grand Rapids: Zondervan, 2003.
Patterson, R. *Nahum, Habakkuk, Zephaniah*. http://www.bible.org.
Taylor, R., and R. Clendenen. *Haggai and Malachi*. Nashville: Broadman & Holman, 2004.